TILTED
DAYS

Shetland

Fair Isle

Orkney

Scotland

TILTED DAYS

A September Gathering of
Fair Isle Poems

by
Shirley Nicholson

Illustrations by Alexa Fitzgibbon

AuthorHouse™ UK
1663 Liberty Drive
Bloomington, IN 47403 USA
www.authorhouse.co.uk
UK TFN: 0800 0148641 (Toll Free inside the UK)
UK Local: 02036 956322 (+44 20 3695 6322 from outside the UK)

This book is printed on acid-free paper.

ISBN: 979-8-8230-8123-8 (sc)
ISBN: 979-8-8230-8122-1 (e)

Print information available on the last page.

Published by AuthorHouse 28/03/2023

authorHOUSE®

Contents

Beginning Days

Looking Beyond the Pilot's Shoulder

The Shipping Forecast
plays in my head like a rhyme

Fair Isle…Fair Isle…Fair Isle
words I've heard since I was young

and now, below, Fair Isle
held in its skin of grass

my first glimpse knife-cut cliff-edge
Sheep Rock: a wren's angled tail feathers

a green brightness in two great seas
small despite the world's knowing.

A Friend Asks
What is the Moon Like?

Where is the lady?
Day after day
night's back drapes
cover the sky.
Perhaps she waits
in the cave
at Kirn O'Skroo,
or her boat
is shipwrecked
on the rocks.
Maybe she hides
behind the tip
of Ward Hill,
or lies in shadow
beyond the faelly daek.
Has she dipped
into the sea
or been whisked
away by wind?
Is she swathed
round a fence post
or asleep in a kennel
with one of the collies,
even tucked away
in the old corn
kiln? Someone
suggests cloud
is the culprit.
Where are you
tonight?

4

Newly Arrived

My back urged forward
by the wind's nagging

west coast on my left
its line looped

like a skipping rope.
What has bitten its edge?

A woman leaves the only shop,
in one hand, her basket,

clutched in the other
a green spike-leaf tuft,

cross-hatched rind
in the wind's bite:

a golden pineapple.

Making the Fire, Lower Leogh

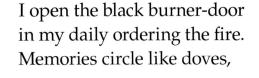

I open the black burner-door
in my daily ordering the fire.
Memories circle like doves,

I clear the ash;
a quiet time to muse
with kindling, card, coal.

After a flickering
in thought, forgotten fires
begin to blaze and glow.

Jimmy's Collie, One-Year-Old Today

Like the swing of a fishing rod
over the water
he'd left his croft

and my nose felt a lick
as I walked.
There he was

red and white,
about to leap again,
pink tongue lolling.

A Few Words with the Wind

My thoughts shuttlelcock
in the air, they toss, they fall.
You prankster, juggler! Back
in my cottage mooring I collect
my thoughts like I'd gather
seeds escaped from a packet,
searching for the tiniest one.

Have you ever imagined
that one day you could pass
me by without coming close,
so my hands are as firm
as hands should be holding
binoculars, and I could stand
pillar still on this green land?

Daddy Long Legs

How they strive
to get out,
flex
their spindle legs,
translucent wings

but outside the porch
is noise and bluster,
intense tantrums
of rain and wind

so they fly to the floor,
tiptoe
to corners
legs hushed, pin thin,
even thinner.

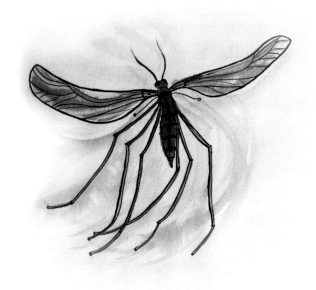

As the Sun Disappears

the sky leaves its blue self

becomes bird-colours

wings outspread

in evening light

gliding above the bay's

open clam shell

a surprise of purple

and rose, even magenta

all gilded

weightless winging

over the ocean's roll

About Sheep

Sheep Rock

As it is covered with herbage on the top, though a literal precipice all round,
the natives contrive to ascend the rock by a place which would make a goat
dizzy, and then drag the sheep up by ropes, though they sometimes carry
a sheep up on their shoulders.

Northern Lights, *The Diary of Sir Walter Scott,* ed. William F. Laughlan
quoted from J.R.Hunter: *Fair Isle, The Archaeology of an Island Community*
pub. The National Trust for Scotland, HMSO 1996.

Seldom a hooftread over the rock edge in their tilted days, a rock edge
on the south side that's a four hundred and fifty foot fall to the sea,
each cranny and ledge taken by seabirds. Gannets plunge, fulmars
engage in guttural conversation. A rock shaped like a cake brought out
from the oven too soon, one side flopped, the other half risen, and a
serrated rock-spine tethering it to the island – it's said a rabbit wouldn't
brave the crossing.

Eleven ewes and a ram feeding on well-flavoured grass. They'd see
their shepherds twice yearly, once after lambing and again for clipping –
and a good day for the men to row their yoals round the east side of
the Rock. First man up would be the test of the chain, as they hoisted
themselves up from the rocky ledge below. The test of the chain.

Sheep grazing on the lush green looking into an infinity of blue, steady
through gales, steady under the stars, winking. Maybe there's no
language to describe them grazing on their slanted rock pedestal. Best
to leave this to the sundown language of sky's flower-petal shades
of primrose, marigold, lilac, fuchsia, foxglove or to the calligraphy of rain,
or the wind's uneven script.

Sage, the White Shetland Ram
for Rachel, Barkland Croft

His fleece a profoundness
of wool fine to finger,
the ragged lines
etched in sunlight.

He decides to loiter
in the path, relax against
the slatted wooden gate,
his magnificent white

leans on turquoise,
horns spiralling ivory.
His shepherdess pauses
on the stone path

beside the low croft.
Two hens strut,
and two lambs nibble
in cabbage, kale, peas.

He turns his head
towards the sun,
eyes dark onyx
set in yellow amber.

15

By the Ruined Mill at Funniquoy

Are they swimmers ready to dive,
these two sheep balanced
on the cliff's blade above sea thrash?

One ewe runs down the rocky incline,
a tilted dash without stumble
to viridian grass by a purling stream.

A lamb grooves into the crevice ledge,
rests there as a sword fits its sheath.

On the Rippack

Sheep-cropped grass wraps the bones of this land.
Rain scrawls the air.
A man and his sheepdog walk an interwoven line
until like a firework flash, the dog leaps
a wire fence, such breadth of space,
lifting with a wind gust like a bird,
the feathery tail a plume against the drained sky.

Island Pulse

Island Pulse

A to and fro between the two
lighthouse bookends, south
to north. One islander explained

there's always jobs to be done,
sheep to be moved, holes
in the road to fill

and when a van breaks down
on the bend by the old corn kiln
an islander mechanic helps

while the driver chats about a merlin
he'd seen, possibly from mainland
Shetland. The reassurance

of the island pace, of cars and vans
driving north and south, far-spaced,
certain as the hour.

The Shetland Flag

Furling and unfurling in the wind,
edges of fabric push against gusts,
stretch at each corner while Britain
unpicks the seam with Europe.

What of Westminster when breeze
lifts this white Nordic cross on blue,
curls round crofts named Setter, Shirva,
Koolin, Nedder Taft, Pund?

Of Araldite and a Straightened Paper Clip

Think through the island skills,
that's what we'll do, you said.
It's a choice between
the skipper of The Good Shepherd
and the man who makes
the straw-backed chairs.
In two small hours a knock
at my door. There you were,
lens fixed in my glasses
the way fingers fit spaces
of a glove, or water fills a cup.

A Conversation

For once words out sound wind's holler in the chapel
entrance. Sentences glide then slowly swoop only to rise
again on a different subject. One woman talks about
a Fair Isle jumper she knitted for a man, an artist. She's
knitting the jumper in her mind as she speaks, choosing
more and more blue wool because he paints using so
much blue. The bird-words fly off in another direction –
she says she was the fourth, the fourth woman on Sheep
Rock, the fourth woman to hoist herself up. Words lift
from her lips.

Kathy's Cushions

Her cushions rest on sofa and chair,
shadowy greys knit with charcoal, gold,
in this cottage among crofting land
beside dykes laden with lichen,
rough grey field stones
adorned with golden yellow,
nature's knit and purl.

Dave Shows us his Sweater

Yarn greets yarn,
a wool conversation
without pause;
no whisker of slip

or spinster yarn,
the finishing precise
as the pattern –

you can almost hear
the knitting rhythm,
a woman steady
in her task

acquamarine, azure,
oatmeal, sand
seamless as the ocean.

Ties

Both hands hold stalks of oats,
make them into a reef knot,
a band to tie each stook
as islanders have done through years,
straw for weaving their chair backs –
under the seat a drawer
to hold balls of knitting wool.

Fishermen tie knots, rope fastened
round the prow, weighted by a stone,
as they haul their yoals
to a noost beyond the beach,
a boat-shaped space dug into earth
so the yoal is safe all winter.

South Light

i

Stairs coil like a watch spring
and my neck cricks from looking up.
I'm a sea snail inside a spiral shell.

ii.

He'd been an assistant keeper,
I feel the easy tread
step after step upwards,
as if he were a child
in a loop of rope
without any pause.

iii.

Who'd imagine a football pitch
spread out by the Atlantic waves?
This green swathe beside the light tower
and all the while mighty wind
filling the players' lungs.
The oyster plant's fleshy leaves,
shining blue flowers, sprawl over
dove-grey pebbles. Looking west
from this balcony, water pools in cupped rocks.
Mothers bring their children,
set back beyond the ocean's growl.

iv.

The ledge where keepers stepped out
to wash the glass panes, the railless ladder
tilted for the final climb to the beacon,
this room where the keeper used to be
on his shift: *Four hours was long enough!*

v.

Clouds pass around the beam like curls of smoke,
reveal caverns in the ebony night,
unlocked space in this dark poetry.
I listen for stillness woven into moments
when wind pauses its roiling, withdraws its lash.
The sheep light up, then are dark again:
the beacon turns, rhythmical as birdsong.

Bird Count

Wings Along the Northern Cliffs

This plying through the spaces,

    through the in-between of cliffs,

each seabird glides in sunlight,

    each shadow a dark bird flying alongside

wind-held looping, wings outspread,

    an unscribbled flight in airborne grace;

white bird shapes, constant cries,

    a backdrop of Prussian-blue sea,

the timing their own,

    back and forth of a story unfolding.

On Malcolm's Head

a rasping   in my left ear   his wingbeat

the sound   a waterproof makes

and the brown bird   so   low   he was inches

from   my random hair   and with   a twist

of my neck   his legs   might have been

in a bird's nest   of   tangle   and   I'd

be   entwined   and   we'd have

come   face   to face   on that hillside

above   the crofting pastures

he   stronger than I   great skua

who lives   in the open space

high up   and he   would have

uttered   his   abrupt   voice   of

  attack.

At Golden Water

There's no mistaking them,
the angle of their heads,

though they might seem
only observers waiting

by unrumpled water,
their stance of ownership

in this northern moorland,
the higher ground.

Stocky red-brown shapes
in late afternoon glow,

great skuas gather
by the unhidden pool

lying in a hollow,
this mirror of the sun.

With the Whooper

In the pasture's dip,
in the land's

half-hidden crease,
a silver gleam –

a pool dug for birds
in the stream's flow

and a large white bird
in this grey quiet

yellow bill bright
beneath a clamour

of clouds. Too late.
The swan's dark eye

is not lazy in this murk.
It spreads its wings

ballerina white,
lifts into the drizzle

followed by a gull,
this white pair

circling together
in murky grey

around South Light,
on over Meoness,

now two black dots
and the pool abandoned.

Fulmar

It hovers
above the stone dyke
daubed in gold
and sage-green lichen,
grey and white feathers
clear beside yellow,
the air above the wall
a waiting room before
it eases downward.
There's a ruckling
of its tail feathers
and as its feet
reach the stone
the bird lifts like a lid
closing then
forced open.
This goes on,
bird pressing down
and lifting,
pressing down again
only to rise, until
a moment of calm,
its nubbed bill
is still, feet
touch the dyke
at last. Then
a swithering
as another gust
surprises
its rump.

Storm Petrel, South Lighthouse

Soot black huddle
feather blackness
on this yellow-ochre balcony
just beneath the beacon –

a bird for the Rangers
to nurture, small thing
in a yellow haven
a found height.

Black bead eyes
tiny black bill, a juvenile
rests here to catch its breath
in the wind's curl.

Sea, Sky, Land and Concrete Slabs

You pause from your bird count,
tell me the Bird Observatory was here,
on this spot above the inlet,
turquoise water, almost white sand –
harbour where *The Good Shepherd*
waits on the slipway.

A thread of sheep tread the wrist
of land from Buness, towards the moorland;
earth's cloth emptied of footprints.
Seabirds lift into the air.
Do they remember?
Do the birds remember?

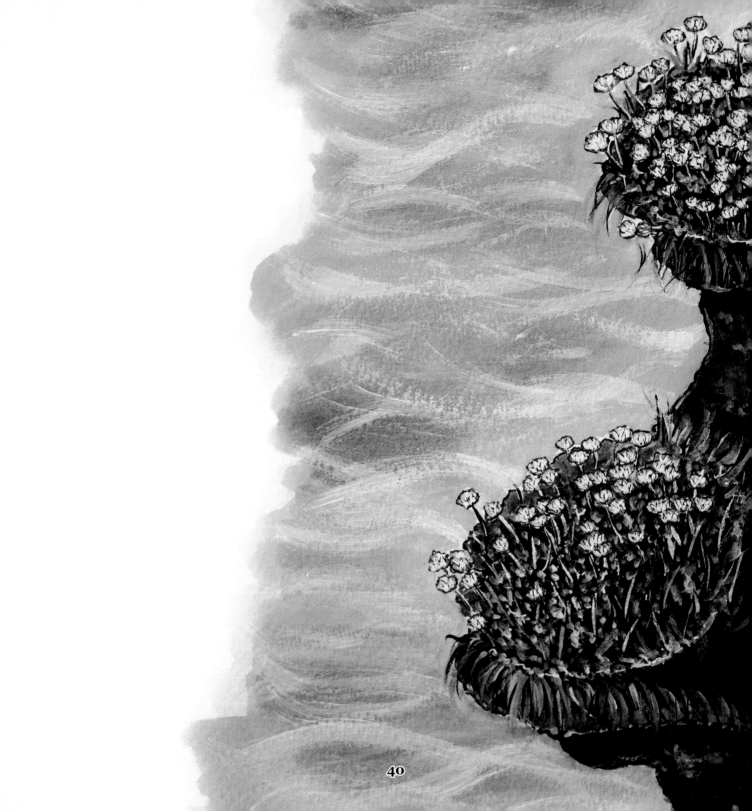

Sea and Land

Blue

Blue takes my hand, commands me
to lean over as far as I dare
on this north-east cliff-edge
in the push of the gale,
shows me the fighting indigo
of sea flecked with seabirds
and whiteness of spume.

Blue lifts my head, tells me
to look at the sky,
a huge bolt of blue unrolling
above our island speck,
cobalt enough to make trousers
for crowds of Dutchmen.

Blue points towards the ocean,
a serene evening blue in the west,
agate breathing silver ripples
with a distant rim of slate;
and when dawn begins to break
Blue calls "Look!"

A ribbon of blue in the north,
an arctic blue rinsed and rinsed,
rises from the ink black —
sky and sea making the land
seem braver for their blueness,
its green more alluring.

The Old Woman of the Hill

She gathers her wide skirt
of grass, moss and bog
hemmed with the stones
of the old faelly daek;

though often hidden
by a bonnet of cloud.
For summer she finds
her sun-stitched shawl,

she mutters to herself,
the bones of her words
heard by great skuas
who low-circle around her –

a weave of purple
and mauve. Her skirt
infolds succulent green
patterned by sheep

robbers, killers who
report back their tales.
Her head is seen
in the loudness of sunlight

in white and brown.
With staff in her hand –
a wired up mast –
she hears the chatter,

knows all the news.
Old as stone this one
looks down from her
tallness, like an older sister

she eyes croft and pasture,
watches the harbour,
observes the planes.
Ages ago they say

she was Beacon Woman
who opened her mouth
in spiralling flame.
Living alone with her troop

of great skuas
sheep munch from her lap,
climb on her shoulders.
We feel her presence

tough as years.
This old island woman shrugs
at the wind, dreams
the colours of the sky.

At South Harbour

I thread bands of turquoise

a blue   dark as midnight

and roar   and roar

from my lion throat

throw   spume on these rocks

play   games with the shag

that fly away

from their sentinel watch

I storm   and bluster

I roll   and roll

batter these cliffs

hurl myself

at obstinate rocks

I'll never give up

I leap   and jump

clear each skerry

make   a spray fountain

that splatters   and stutters

like a writhing snake

I curl   and twist –

a fearsome creature

I foam   and froth –

what treasures   I hide

great shoals of fish

and   shipwrecks –

a Viking longboat

the Canadia   even

the flagship El Gran Grifon

from the Armada   how close

I held the cries   the tears –

in a welter of waves

I'll make another   rush

for the pebbled shore

where sheep chew kelp

dangling in ribbons

from their mouths

this island   is mine

held in my hands   I shine

these rocks till

they gleam   like metal

sparkle   like jet

and the grey seals –

their cannon ball heads –

cannot outshine

the lustre

this ink black   wetness

in luminous light

Walking Above Klinger's Geo

rain light   rain slant

sheen of cotton grass   sea rage   wing curve

      lark lift   mud shine   foot slip

bog clump   wind blast

      sheep's bit blue   cliff drop

wool tuft   sheep tracks   thrift pink.

cloud umbrella   smell of wind

grass nibbled   slope bevel

      wind thrust

      plashy earth underfoot

dark rock

      sea sparkle

Some Small September Things

Sea mayweed
clasps wispy leaves
in spray's toss;

rose-pink thrift –
green pincushions
frugal on cliff ledges –

resists the wind.
Fingers of tormentil
scatter yellow

near fluted silver leaf
as the island wren bobs
along the field-edge,

tail upturned.
The sun dips its flare
into the Atlantic

and a small van
pootles along
this puddled track;

somehow its tyres
miss the few
blushed daisies.

From One of the Natural Springs

concealed by tufts

of grass and bog

flowing glass-clear in the moorland

quicksilver movement

where early settlers dwelled

bird of the earth

flies over pebble and stone

fresh as a new day

calling down light

A Plastic Bottle and a Mermaid's Purse

Discarded from a fishing boat
or one of the cruise ships,
a bottle, bright orange cap
tight on the plastic rim
and in bold yellow lettering:
Lucozade.

Lodged in slate-grey pebbles
a pouch cast up from the Atlantic
fashioned like leatherwork,
this small thing caught in sunlight,
a tendril at each corner
to hook the ebony purse to seaweed.

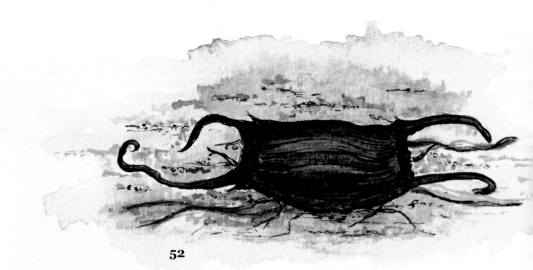

Asking

i.
And what of the trees?
Do their ghosts pass among
these gales, seedlings

that tried to grow and failed?
Are rootless wanderers
walking through these winds

spreading their branches,
an unseen lattice
stretched above us?

ii.
If trees grew here,
when autumn came
leaves would fly like birds
in these winds, they'd rise
and the sky filled
with murmurations,
their twist and turn,
swoop and swirl.

Island Vespers

The sky gathers her colour choir
calling them for choral evensong
floating threads and drifts,
stray mauves and amber,
gleams of deep topaz –
no need to find a pew
or try to reach some holiness.
Singing fills the transept in the west.

Past and Present Celebrated

The *Lessing* Remembered, 1868

I'm thinking of the figurines
in the cottage, ladies with pink shawls,
full-brimmed hats, floral dresses
and sirs with white breeches, frock coats,
cravats, brown leather boots.
So much to tell, but their words
locked in porcelain. Salvage
from the *Lessing* bound for New York,
trapped in this geo, knotted in rocks,
unable to slip away from the land,
this knob of land set in two tiger seas.
Island necklaced by shipwreck,
where two seas meet, place
of different tides, cross-currents,
and she, in this crossfire,
the sea unable to pull her away,
the rocks holding her in their grip.
They were the fortunate ones,
these travellers from Bremen
rescued by brave islanders.
What of the other ships
sailing these sea passages?
The sky turns opal, its fire
burns over wave-hidden disasters.
An island skipper says
I only go to sea on the sea's terms.

Unearthly

Listen.
It floats across the tidal pool
held by two backbones of rock,
a tranquil place, tide ebbing beyond
clear blue specks among fleshy blue-green
leaves: the oyster plant sprawl
on a shingle swathe,
singing   singing   drifts
hollow above the petals.
Grey mist creeps landward,
a sea elegy held in air.
An invisible hand bears it to our ears.

As Winds Push Clouds Eastwards

A drifting thicket of pewter,
an elephant-grey sea;
a meadow pipit calls in the rain-shimmer –
gloss of sudden afternoon sun.
Fence wires weep light,
stretch to the graveyard
by winter noosts at South Harbour,
beside waves thrashing dark rock.
Headstones defy storms,
pages of island history written
there by the sea...Jerome Eunson,
Stewart and Agnes Eunson,
Jane and George Stout, Margaret Stout,
Jacobina Wilson, James Wilson,
Stewart and Mary Eunson
and their family.

Waiting

i.

It's time to see gold and brown,
watch colours change,

smell the wood smoke of bonfires;
time to shed the old, prepare

for the new. Yet green still
spills everywhere – grass green,

shadow greens, the trilling green
of bushes alive with birds.

No fruit dangles from boughs
though someone said she'd eaten

a pear the other day, a pear
so juicy it danced in her mouth,

conservatory grown. They tell me
the geese are on their way.

ii.

A faint guttural sound
carries across the sea,

amplified through the air.
Black spots in the sky

become beaks and wings,
a procession over the island

thrusting forward,
a fresh energy in the sky.

They hold their line, turn
as they reach the west coast,

curve and curve again
before their descent

each bird's outline
clear in evening shine

honking in the wind,
wings full of travel.

By afternoon the sky
unfolds dark ripples,

three flocks, their flight paths
pressing forward to cliffs

that leap from the sea,
skeins streaming

as the sky unravels
its bird-yarns.

Red Admiral

Flickering brilliance in a windless hour,

it basks in warm sunlight

beside green fields and grazing sheep.

Flame-red, white and velvet black

outshine the turquoise cottage wall,

a colour-shout after days of cold.

Even the sea's roar in Hesti Geo

diminished by this shining.

Song of the Scythe

too much grass today
for the tractor blade so
tchshshshsh tchshshshsh
take a stretch of oats
cut them low down
tchshshsh tchshshsh
hold my blade level
keep a steady rhythm
tchshshsh tchshshsh
my blade is curved
my blade is strong
tchshshsh tchshshsh
gather handfuls of stalks
knot them together
tchshshsh tchshshsh
with these knotted cords
bind each stook
tchshshsh tchshshsh
prop up the stooks
six by six, six by six
tchshshsh tchshshsh
lean them at angles
so rain will fall away
tchshshsh tchshshsh
so rain will fall away
and wind cannot push
tchshshsh tchshshsh
o, my blade is curved
my blade is strong
tchshshsh tchshshsh
tchshshsh tchshshsh.

Hymn of Island Paths

Praise the path of the sun
as it silvers the sea,
defines each wave.

Praise paths of sheep,
trails in the earth,
centuries trodden.

Praise paths of people,
their walk and amble,
the friendly stiles.

Praise paths of the sea,
hidden in gales,
seen in calm waters.

Praise paths of the wind,
its slap and gust,
fight and frolic.

Praise paths of wool,
the coloured yarns,
island designs.

Praise paths of birds
weaving their patterns,
coming, leaving.

Praise paths
as they meet,
as they part.

Cooking Salmon in the Kitchen

Rustlings in the rugosa bushes
near the kitchen window
where nets hang for Rangers

to ring and count birds,
and a lime-green knife
lies on the draining board

beside a fillet of salmon
from mainland Shetland,
a delicious pink. I've learnt

to listen to island talk,
learn when the boat sails
or cannot make it in the wind;

learnt to be quick to the shop
when the boat has harboured
in North Haven,

their *Good Shepherd IV* –
bringer and mover,
in white, red, blue.

On the Last Night

When the wind had disappeared
in a vanish as sudden
as a genie in a puff of smoke

and the door didn't lurch
on its hinge when opened,
and it was possible to stand

in the dark without being
thrust back into the croft,
then I could walk in the night,

in a living brightness of stars,
a diamond-light sparkle,
and there she rested

on Meoness, poised like a gull
stopped in low flight.
Had I ever seen gold like this?

Sea Glass

From time to time
they toss pieces of glass
into the waves
so the sea may return
these fragments
transformed,
each shard
a type of butterfly
emerging
from its chrysalis
in far-away blues,
frost white, ice light,
peat browns,
in the green of forests,
in green mist-quiet.

Sunset

An opening in the clouds,
a beckoning
through a strange glow
lemon bright,
touched by peach.

The sky a fabric woven
in shades of indigo
and mauve, strands
of blossom pink and saffron.
Brushstrokes

of violet cloud-wisps
drift across the Atlantic,
over waves haloed in light.
What of the five birds –
pink-footed geese –

which flew on the easterly
a few hours ago,
landed on the slope?
They stand in the field
each wing outlined.

The Chapel Bell Rings

Birds come and go as they've done for years and years
though at ground level there's an unspoken fear. Like a
bird the *Good Shepherd IV* needs to come and go,
the small plane too with its magical route over outlying islands.

On this isle open wide to the sky, no overhang of tree,
mountain, or tall buildings, there's a new thing hidden
under the moss-covered stone of each person's thought.

A long time since the chapel bell has been heard across
the island the Fair Isle newspaper writes. Time of constraints,
shadows on the island's centuries-long close-knittedness.
Time of concern over visitors, shadows on the islanders'
spirit of welcome that shines like sun lighting the ocean.

But the chapel bell rings. Sound of coming together. It rings.

A Fair Isle Lullaby

Fridarey, Fridarey, island of sheep,
Fridarey, Fridarey, sleep my child, sleep.
Let the land wrap you round,
Let this wool keep you warm,
Let the sky sing you songs,
May you nest free from harm.
Fridarey, Fridarey, island of sheep,
Fridarey, Fridarey, sleep my child sleep.

A Fair Isle Lullaby

Music: Liam Paul
Words: Shirley Nicholson

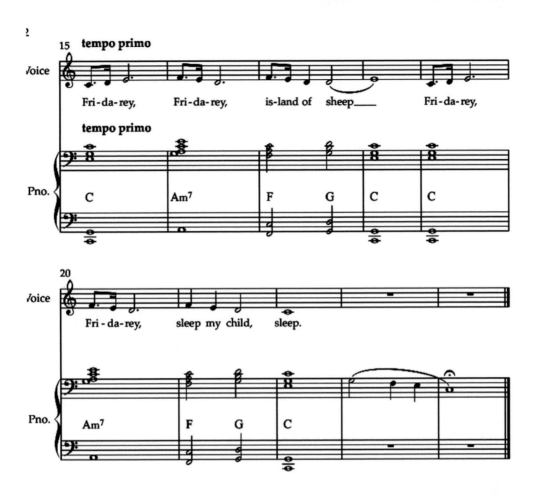

Fridarey: plausibly a derivation of Farey (ON faar-ey) with the same root as Faroe, meaning 'island of sheep'. (Hunter, J.R. Fair Isle)

Fridarey pronounced *Free-da-ray*, emphasis on *Free*

Notes

The first inhabitants on the island came more than six thousand years ago. (see *Fair Isle Through the Seasons* by Malachy Tallack and Roger Riddington.) Archaeological evidence includes late-Neolithic land divisions; Bronze Age burnt mounds and the promontory Iron Age fort at Landberg.

In recent years the ornithologist George Waterson bought the island in 1948, sold the island to its present owners the National Trust for Scotland in 1954.

p. 4   The faelly-daek is an old division of land separating cultivated land and communal grazing. Pronounced failee dik see https://www.shetlanddialect.org.uk/john-j-grahams-shetland-dictionary.php?word=709

p. 7   Leogh is pronounced low.

p. 10   In many parts of the world a Daddy Long Legs is the name of a spider, but in the UK a Daddy Long Legs is another name for the Crane Fly.

p. 14   The last sheep were taken off the Rock in 1977. (See *Fair Isle: A Photographic History* by George Waterson and Jean Jones.)

p. 16   There was a small group of watermills with horizontal wheels at Funniquoy, by the Burn of Gilsetter.

p. 21   Norse settlers took control of the island from around the early eighth century until the official handover to Scotland in 1469.

              The Shetland flag was developed in 1969 to celebrate the 500th anniversary of Shetland becoming part of Scotland and the five hundred years before as part of Norway. The flag celebrates Shetland's

Norse and Scottish history, carrying the Scandinavian cross alongside the colours of the Scottish saltire.

p. 25   This jumper had been knitted for Stewart Wilson, a minister in the Church of Scotland. Originally from a long line of islanders he returned to the island when he retired. Stewart was an artist and one of his paintings was on the wall in Dave and Josie's home. This painting inspired Triona Thomson to kit the jumper. When Stewart passed away his son offered this treasure to Dave as Dave and his father were of similar build.

p. 26   The Fair Isle yoal was an echo of the boats used by the Norsemen, long narrow boats, a relative of the Ness yoal from mainland Shetland.

p. 27   There are two lighthouses on the island, one in the north (Skroo) and one in the south (Skaddan). David Stevenson and Charles Stevenson, cousins of Robert Louis Stevenson, built both of these. South Light was operational in 1892 and was the last Scottish manned lighthouse to be automated in 1998.

p. 38   While I was on the island three Rangers were being employed by the Fair Isle Bird Observatory Trust. I came across them ringing and counting birds.

p. 39   George Waterson visited the island in 1935 and longed for a bird observatory to be built. In August 1948 his wishes were realised and a bird observatory opened. This was refurbished in 1998/9. Later a new observatory was built and opened in 2010. Tragically, there was a fire in March 2019 and the second observatory was burnt down. The Fair Isle Bird Observatory Trust has been raising funds to build a new bird observatory. The building was begun in 2022, and it's hoped it will be completed at the end of 2023 or early 2024.

p. 44　Ward Hill is the only hill and rises in the communal grazing land beyond the division of the faelly daek (see Notes p. 4). The pure Shetland sheep graze here. Islanders often refer to the communal grazing area as "the hill".

p. 46　In the case of the *El Gran Grifon*, a flagship of the Spanish Armada's supply squadron, all but seven of the men reached shore safely when the ship became wedged against the cliff at Stroms Heelor, 1588. (See *Standing Into Danger: Shipwrecks of Fair Isle* by Anne Sinclair.) The same book refers to the wreck of a Viking longship in AD.900. Though many were lost in shipwreck after shipwreck those on board the *Canadia* in 1915 were all rescued. (See *Standing Into Danger*.)

p. 49　Geo pronounced GYO

p. 50　This wren is a species found nowhere else in Europe except on Fair Isle.

p. 56　The *Lessing* was carrying German emigrants to New York. She was wrecked in Klavers Geo. The islanders saved all the four hundred and sixty five people on board.

p. 58　A kirk by the graveyard has been demolished. Eunson pronounced YUN-son.

p. 58　Geo pronounced GYO.

p. 65　Traditional Fair Isle way of tying knots with the corn.

p. 70　A Ranger said that occasionally islanders throw glass into the sea hoping that the sea will return it as sea glass.

p. 72　The Church of Scotland kirk built in the late nineteenth century was closed and services are now held in the Methodist Chapel, beside the Museum, above South Harbour.

Acknowledgements

Thanks to the friends and family who encouraged me in this venture and thanks to Marie Naughton for keeping in touch with me during my stay on the island.

At South Harbour was first published in BlueHouse Journal, 2020.

Thanks to the islanders who made me feel welcome – to Josie Wennekes and Dave Brackenbury, Neil Thompson, the chapel community, Fiona and Robert Mitchell, Jimmy Stout and Glen, and thanks to Amy for telling me about the wind. Enormous appreciation to Rachel Challoner for showing me round her croft and answering endless questions.

Thanks to Julie Jarman for her support and to Daphne Laura Richardson for her invaluable advice. Thanks to Jenny Fox and Charlie Perry.

Thanks to Gilian Allnutt for the assignment to write a lullaby at a poetry workshop and to Liam Paul (www.liammcclair.com) for composing the music.

Thanks to Laurie Goodlad for her interest and endorsement. Thanks to her also for introducing me to the artist Alexa Fitzgibbon. I so appreciate that Alexa agreed to do these illustrations.

My thanks to John McAuliffe for his encouragement and endorsement.

Most grateful thanks to Alicia Stubbersfield for her friendship, for her close reading of the poems and for her real interest in all that I was learning about the island.

Special Thanks

This collection of poems arises from my Creative Residency on Fair Isle during September 2020, made possible through Fair Isle Studio. The Residency provides development space for artists, makers, designers, writers, musicians, researchers and anyone seeking concentrated time for their creative practice.

Covid regulations meant that the usual hum of community activity was silenced. The poems reflect that I was unable to meet many people and, sadly, was not able to see much of the wonderful knitting. In spite of this, the underlying sense of community was always present and I am very grateful for the friendship I was able to find in these exceptional circumstances. It was a special month.

Biographical Notes

Shirley Nicholson has an enduring love for Scotland fostered by Scottish parents, childhood summers in Edinburgh with grandparents and special time with an artist aunt in the Dumfriesshire countryside – an aunt who initiated her continuing love for the Scottish islands. Her poems have appeared in various anthologies and magazines. One of her poems was chosen for Poems on the Move in 2021 and again in 2022 and she participated in two London Gardens' poetry residencies. She holds an MA in Creative Writing from the Centre for New Writing, University of Manchester and served on the Poets and Players advisory group for a number of years. Shirley brought her aunt's wartime diary to publication, *The Milk Lady at New Park Farm*, a diary about working on the land during World War Two.

Alexa Fitzgibbon is a Franco-British artist who has been living in Shetland for over ten years. A lot of her work is inspired by her love for Shetland's particular landscapes, light and skies, but also by its folklore and storytelling history.

Printed in the United States
by Baker & Taylor Publisher Services